Inside the Brain

Rufus Bellamy

A⁺

First published in 2004 by Franklin Watts
96 Leonard Street, London EC2A 4XD

Franklin Watts Australia
45–51 Huntley Street, Alexandria, NSW 2015
This edition published under license from Franklin Watts. All rights reserved.

Series editor: Adrian Cole
Series design: White Design
Art director: Jonathan Hair
Picture research: Diana Morris
Educational consultant: Peter Riley
Medical consultant: Dr. Gabrielle Murphy

Published in the United States by Smart Apple Media
1980 Lookout Drive, North Mankato, Minnesota 56003

Library of Congress Control Number: 2004102616

ISBN 1-58430-462-7

2 4 6 8 9 7 5 3 1

Acknowledgments:

Bettmann/Corbis: 15bl. Dee Breger/SPL: 26t. BSIP, Keene/SPL: 16b.
Chris Clarke/Newsflash/Pressnet/Topham: 11b. CNRI/SPL: 12b. Bob
Daemmrich/The Image Works/Topham: 7b, 26b, 27b. Klaus
Guldbrandsen/SPL: 7t. Ted Horowitz/Corbis: 28t. Jacksonville
Courier/The Image Works/Topham: 8t. Gabe Palmer/Corbis: 5t. Alfred
Pasieka/SPL: 4t. Philippe Plailly/SPL: 25b. SPL: 10t. Geoff Tompkinson/SPL:
20t. UPPA Ltd/Topham: 20b. Alesandro Vinnini/Corbis Sygma: 5b.
Wellcome Dept of Cognative Neurology/SPL: 15br.
Bo Zaunders/Corbis:23t. Zephyr/SPL: 13b.

Contents

The brain controls
the body

The brain weighs only about 3.1 pounds (1.4 kg), but it controls our movement, keeps the body functioning properly, and lets us understand and communicate with the world around us.

Powerful network
The brain is made up of many billions of nerve cells called neurons that link together into a highly complicated network. The brain functions 24 hours a day and is much more powerful than any computer that has ever been made.

Skull bone
protects the brain

Cerebrum
(see page 13)

Spinal link

This scan clearly shows the connection between the brain and the spinal cord, which runs from the base of the brain down the back.

Linked to the body
The brain is joined to the spinal cord, which runs down the back. Both are linked to the body through a network of nerves. Information about what is happening inside and outside the body travels to the brain and spinal cord along these nerves. Nerves also carry instructions from the brain and spinal cord to the body.

Many functions
The brain controls a range of functions, from movement to the production of feelings and emotions. Different parts of the brain do specific jobs, but many functions, such as thinking, involve different areas acting together.

Skull cutaway
The brain is made of soft tissue. It is protected by the hard, bony skull.

THE BRAIN IN ACTION

Nerve impulses move continuously around the network of neurons that make up the brain. As this happens, the brain produces tiny electrical signals called brain waves. Brain waves can be detected by a machine called an electroencephalograph (EEG). Scientists can look at the different types of waves and determine what the brain is doing and whether it is healthy.

Exam pressure

During an exam, the brain produces a lot of brain waves as it recalls information and thinks.

Chemical links

The nerves are not the only route through which the brain controls the body. The brain is also linked to the endocrine system (*see pages 26–27*). This produces chemicals, called hormones (*see pages 28–29*), that influence things such as our emotions and food digestion. The brain and the endocrine system work together to make sure that all these things happen properly.

Day-to-day life

The people here are using their brains to control almost all of their activities, including walking and talking.

The nervous system links the
brain and the body

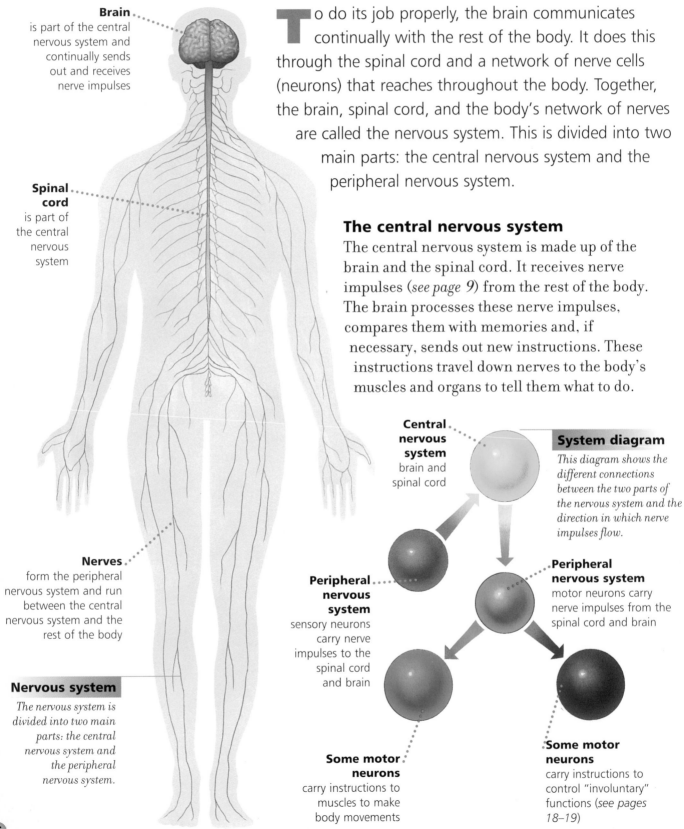

Brain is part of the central nervous system and continually sends out and receives nerve impulses

Spinal cord is part of the central nervous system

Nerves form the peripheral nervous system and run between the central nervous system and the rest of the body

Nervous system

The nervous system is divided into two main parts: the central nervous system and the peripheral nervous system.

To do its job properly, the brain communicates continually with the rest of the body. It does this through the spinal cord and a network of nerve cells (neurons) that reaches throughout the body. Together, the brain, spinal cord, and the body's network of nerves are called the nervous system. This is divided into two main parts: the central nervous system and the peripheral nervous system.

The central nervous system

The central nervous system is made up of the brain and the spinal cord. It receives nerve impulses (*see page 9*) from the rest of the body. The brain processes these nerve impulses, compares them with memories and, if necessary, sends out new instructions. These instructions travel down nerves to the body's muscles and organs to tell them what to do.

Central nervous system brain and spinal cord

System diagram

This diagram shows the different connections between the two parts of the nervous system and the direction in which nerve impulses flow.

Peripheral nervous system sensory neurons carry nerve impulses to the spinal cord and brain

Peripheral nervous system motor neurons carry nerve impulses from the spinal cord and brain

Some motor neurons carry instructions to muscles to make body movements

Some motor neurons carry instructions to control "involuntary" functions (*see pages 18–19*)

The peripheral nervous system

The peripheral nervous system is made up of the nerves that run to and from the central nervous system. The peripheral nervous system carries nerve impulses from sensory neurons all over the body. The peripheral nervous system also carries the instructions the central nervous system sends out to the rest of the body via motor neurons. When these impulses get to the body's muscles and organs, they produce a response.

Information carriers

Nerves of the peripheral nervous system, like the ones above, carry nerve impulses all over the body and forge a link between the body and the central nervous system.

A home run

Your nervous system provides you with all the information you need to hit the ball and hopefully to get a home run.

THE NERVOUS SYSTEM IN ACTION

The nervous system allows you to respond to situations. For example, in a game of baseball, your eyes and ears and other sense organs continually send nerve impulses along sensory neurons to your brain. Your brain compares these nerve impulses to its memories of games you have played. It then sends new nerve impulses, at the right time, via the spinal cord and peripheral nervous system to your arm muscles, instructing them to move. When these instructions reach your arms, you swing the bat and hopefully hit a home run.

Nerves are the body's
communication system

Nerves are the "wires" that link the central nervous system to the rest of the body. There are more than 60 miles (100 km) of nerves in the body, and they reach all parts of the skin, internal organs, and muscles. Nerves can be up to an inch (2 cm) thick, or thinner than a hair. They are covered in a sheath and contain bundles of nerve cells called neurons.

Axon terminals
where the motor neuron meets muscle fiber

Making a connection
Nerves are like the wires of a telephone network. They enable the brain to stay in touch with the body.

Nerve fiber or axon

Dendrites
carry nerve impulses from other neurons toward the cell body

Cell body
contains the cell's nucleus or "control center"

Neurons

Neurons are long cells that come in all different shapes and sizes. All of them have three main parts: a cell body, dendrites, and an axon (or nerve fiber).

Sensory and motor neurons

There are two types of neuron in the peripheral nervous system: sensory neurons and motor neurons. Sensory neurons carry information to the central nervous system about what is happening inside and outside the body. Motor neurons carry instructions from the central nervous system to muscles and organs.

A motor neuron
Nerve impulses from the brain and spinal cord travel only in one direction along a motor neuron.

Old cells

Most cells in the body "die" and are replaced. However, neurons (especially those in the brain and spinal cord) are very different. Most last a lifetime and are not normally replaced if they "die" as a result of old age, injury, or disease. This means that neurons are among the oldest cells in the body, and that as we age, we have fewer neurons.

Inside a nerve

Nerves, like the one shown here, usually contain both motor and sensory neurons.

Outer sheath
protects the bundles of neurons

Motor neuron
see opposite page

Sensory receptor
responds to stimuli, such as light or temperature

Blood vessel
supplies oxygen and nutrients to the nerve

Sensory neuron
carries nerve impulses from the sense receptor to the central nervous system

Muscle fiber

Axon terminals

Motor neuron

Sensory neuron

Direction of nerve impulses

Synapse
is a gap that chemical messages pass across

ELECTRICAL SIGNALS

Neurons carry information and instructions in the form of nerve impulses. A nerve impulse is an electrical signal that travels along a neuron (always in the same direction). This happens when a sensory receptor or dendrite at the end of the nerve is stimulated. The brain analyzes nerve impulses it receives and sends out new nerve impulses to control the body.
  Neurons meet at junctions called synapses, but they do not touch. When a nerve impulse reaches a synapse, chemicals are released. These chemicals cross the gap and start a nerve impulse in the next neuron.

Nerve impulse in action

Nerve impulses travel along neurons in only one direction. Here, an impulse travels from a sensory receptor to a motor neuron in a reflex action (see page 11).

The spinal cord is the body's
communication highway

The spinal cord is a tube of nervous tissue that runs down the back of the body from the base of the brain to the lower back. It is the main communication highway between the brain and the rest of the body. The spinal cord carries nerve impulses to and from the brain. These impulses enter and leave the spinal cord through nerves, which branch off and run throughout the body. The spinal cord also plays an important role in coordinating the body's activity (*see opposite page*).

Skull (rear)
is a bony case that protects the brain

The highway
Nerve impulses travel up and down the spinal cord, carrying messages to and from the body.

Spinal cord cross-section
The "H"-shaped core of the spinal cord (colored red) contains association neurons.

Spinal cord
is a tube of nervous tissue

Spinal nerves
branch off and run throughout the body

Protected tissue

The spinal cord is well-protected by the backbone, which is made up of a column of bones called vertebrae. Each vertebra has a hole running through it. Together, these holes make up a tunnel through which the spinal cord runs. The spinal cord is also surrounded by fluid and protected by membranes.

Membranes
surround the spinal cord

Vertebrae
form a column of bones

Backbone (side view)
The nervous tissue of the spinal cord is protected by three membranes and the bony vertebrae, which form the backbone.

Spinal nerves

Spinal nerves attach to the spinal cord through gaps between each vertebra. These nerves contain sensory and motor neurons. Most sensory neurons enter the back of the spinal cord, while most motor neurons leave at the front.

Spinal cord sections

Inside the spinal cord there are two main areas. The first is an inner, "H"-shaped core, mainly made up of association neurons (*see below*). These link the spinal nerves to other nerve fibers. The second area is the outer part of the spinal cord. It is mainly made up of nerve fibers that carry nerve impulses up and down the spinal cord.

Inner layer
is "H"-shaped and contains association neurons

Outer layer
is made up of nerve fibers

Spinal nerve

Spinal nerve

Protective membranes

Reflex action

This is how pain causes the spinal cord to "short circuit," which allows the body to respond quickly.

Spinal cord cutaway

The nervous tissue of the spinal cord forms two clearly defined areas.

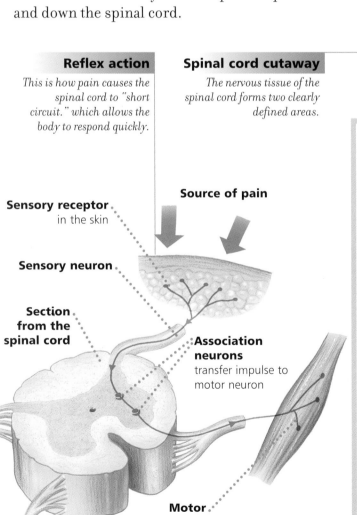

Sensory receptor
in the skin

Source of pain

Sensory neuron

Section from the spinal cord

Association neurons
transfer impulse to motor neuron

Motor neuron
in muscle

REFLEX ACTIONS

Many actions in the body happen automatically without you having to think about them. When you touch something, such as a hot iron or a scary spider, you pull your hand away from it quickly. These "reflex" actions are coordinated by the spinal cord. During a reflex action, nerve impulses enter the spinal cord and are immediately directed back out of the spinal cord down a motor neuron. This "short circuit" allows the body to respond to fear, pain, or danger by making muscles move quickly.

The brain is the body's
control center

The brain is the control center of the body and the place where thoughts take place and memories are stored. It is very soft and sits securely inside the skull. The brain is covered in tough protective membranes and also bathed in fluid, which supports it and protects it from damage. The brain is divided into three main areas: the brainstem, cerebellum, and forebrain.

Cerebrum
is part of the forebrain
(*see opposite page*)

Thalamus
is part of the
forebrain that sends
nerve impulses to the
cerebral cortex
(*see page 14*)

Corpus callosum
the bridge that connects
two halves of the cerebrum

Hypothalamus
is part of the
forebrain

Brainstem
transfers nerve impulses
between the brain and
the spinal cord

Cerebellum
controls
movement
and balance

Spinal cord
(*see pages 10–11*)

Brain blood vessels
The brain needs a lot of oxygen and nutrients to keep it functioning properly. Shown here in red are the blood vessels that supply the brain.

Brain areas
This cutaway shows the three main areas: the brainstem, cerebellum, and the forebrain.

Special supply
The walls of the blood vessels that supply the brain form a barrier between the blood and the brain. This is so that no poisonous or foreign substances can get into the brain and damage it.

The forebrain
The forebrain has four distinct parts: the cerebrum (*see opposite page*), thalamus, hypothalamus, and the limbic system. The thalamus recognizes and sorts information that arrives in the brain and relays it to areas of the cerebrum. The hypothalamus (*see pages 19 and 27*) helps regulate many of the body's "involuntary" functions, such as the control of body temperature. The limbic system (*see pages 22–23*) controls instincts and emotions.

This view from the front of the cerebrum clearly shows the layers of gray and white matter.

White matter
is mainly made up of nerve fibers that link the cerebral cortex to the rest of the brain

Gray matter (cerebral cortex)
is rich in nerve cells

The largest part of the brain

The cerebrum is the largest part of the brain. It is where information is processed, where thought takes place, where memories are stored, and decisions are made. The left and right side of the cerebrum are linked by a "bridge" called the corpus callosum. Each side has a slightly different role (*see below*). The outer part of the cerebrum is called "gray matter" (the cerebral cortex), and the inner layer is called "white matter."

The cerebellum

The cerebellum is part of the brain that works with the cerebrum to regulate smooth body movements. It also helps to make sure that we stay balanced. Without the cerebellum, we would not be able to properly control the body.

LEFT AND RIGHT

The left and right sides of the brain control the opposite sides of the body. The two sides also have a number of specific functions. Musical and other artistic, creative, and imaginative skills are mainly the responsibility of the right, while mathematical and speech skills are mainly the responsibility of the left. In most people, fine control of the hand is also controlled by the left, which is why most people are right-handed.

Control crossover

The left or right side of the brain receives sensory information from the opposite side of the body and also sends instructions to muscles on the opposite side of the body.

Two halves

The two halves of the cerebrum, shown here, are often called hemispheres.

The brain receives and
processes information

The brain is continually bombarded with nerve impulses from sense organs, such as the eyes, ears, and skin. Information also comes from receptors inside the body. All of this information is carried to the brain via the nerves of the peripheral nervous system and the spinal cord.

The cerebral cortex

Information is directed to different areas of the brain via the thalamus. For example, most of the sensory information the brain receives is processed by the surface layer of the cerebrum—the cerebral cortex. Areas in the middle and side of the cerebral cortex receive information about touch, taste, hearing, and smell. Information from the eyes goes to an area at the back of the cerebrum called the visual cortex.

Parietal lobe
receives impulses from
touch and pain receptors

**Occipital lobe
(visual cortex)**
receives and analyzes
impulses from
the eyes

Frontal lobe
controls speech
and thought
(see page 21)

Temporal lobe
receives and
analyzes impulses
from the ears

Areas of the brain (external)
*The surface of the brain—the cerebral
cortex—is divided into four main lobes.*

Judo practice
*These judo students use the information
sent to their brains from different sense
organs to help overcome their opponents.*

Understanding nerve impulses

To understand what is happening, the brain decodes nerve impulses, analyzes them, and compares them with stored memories. This information becomes the "sensations" we experience. For example, we use information from the nose in order to understand our surroundings and to protect the body—if food has a bad smell we might decide not to eat it.

Brain response

Once the brain has analyzed and understood the information, it makes decisions based on that information. It also stores the information it has received as memories (*see pages 24–25*) and sends instructions out to the body to respond.

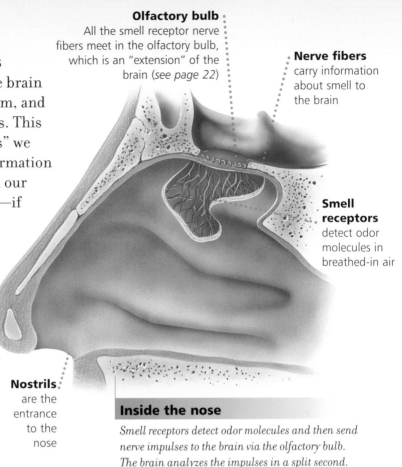

Olfactory bulb
All the smell receptor nerve fibers meet in the olfactory bulb, which is an "extension" of the brain (*see page 22*)

Nerve fibers
carry information about smell to the brain

Smell receptors
detect odor molecules in breathed-in air

Nostrils
are the entrance to the nose

Inside the nose

Smell receptors detect odor molecules and then send nerve impulses to the brain via the olfactory bulb. The brain analyzes the impulses in a split second.

MAPPING THE BRAIN

The modern, scientific approach to understanding the brain started in the late 19th century, when a French scientist named Pierre Broca investigated the brains of people who had speech problems. He found that a certain area of their brains had been damaged by disease. Other scientists looked at what happened when they cut into the brains of some patients or stimulated the brains of animals with electricity. In this way, the function of different parts of the brain began to be uncovered.

Brain scans

Since early "brain maps" (see left), technology has developed so that we can take special images of brain activity.

Movement is coordinated by
the brain

One of the most important things that the central nervous system does is to control movement. Every time we reach for something, walk, or say a word, the central nervous system controls and coordinates the action of the body muscles to make the movement happen.

Motor control

The motor area of the cerebrum controls most complex movements. It lies in the middle and to the side of the cerebral cortex (*see page 21*). Different areas of this part of the brain control the movement of different parts of the body. Parts of the body that perform precise movements have more of this space devoted to them.

PARALYSIS

Paralysis happens when a person cannot move some or all of their muscles. It can occur if the brain is damaged by injury or if its blood supply is cut off temporarily. It also happens if the spinal cord is damaged and nerve impulses cannot travel between the brain and muscles. Diseases, such as polio, can also affect the nervous system and cause paralysis. Once the spinal cord or the brain is damaged, the cells usually cannot be repaired.

Paraolympian

Paralysis does not mean that the brain stops working. This athlete is taking part in the Paraolympic Games, which are held every four years.

Learning to move

Many movements are complicated, involving the use of many muscles. Key movements, such as walking, are learned in childhood. "Programs" for different types of movement are stored in the brain, particularly in the cerebellum (*see page 12*). These programs are relayed to the cerebral cortex when we decide to move.

Skipping

Skipping may seem simple, but it involves highly coordinated, precisely timed movements of the body.

Keep practicing

Movements, such as those used for bowling, have to be learned. If they are practiced, the brain memorizes what has to be done and gets better at repeating it.

Cerebellum

The cerebellum is vital in controlling movement and ensuring that our movements are smooth and accurate. It also helps control our posture and keeps us balanced.

Coordinating movements

To coordinate muscle movement, the brain continually monitors the information it receives from sensors all over the body. The main sensors are inside the ear (which send nerve impulses about body position and balance) and inside muscles and tendons (which send nerve impulses about muscle movement and position). This information goes to the cerebellum, where it is processed and then sent to the motor areas of the cerebrum. The brain then sends out new instructions that "fine tune" the body's movement.

The nervous system controls
body functions

The nervous system controls many body functions without us being aware of it. For example, it coordinates the muscles of the digestive system as they move food along inside the body. The part of the nervous system that controls these "involuntary" functions is called the autonomic nervous system.

Food ball
is made up of chewed and crushed food

Peristalsis

Muscles of the digestive system relax and contract forming a wave-like action called peristalsis. It is one function controlled by the autonomic nervous system.

Stomach
churns chewed food into a runny mixture

Small intestine
absorbs nutrients from food

Muscle wall
contracts and relaxes, slowly moving the food ball toward the stomach

Autonomic nervous system

The autonomic nervous system helps control everything from heart rate and breathing to digestion and body temperature (*see opposite page*). It helps regulate how the organs in the body perform and helps to make sure everything inside the body works properly. The autonomic nervous system helps coordinate the activity of many parts of the body. For example, when we run, the autonomic nervous system automatically speeds up the heart rate, increases blood pressure, and slows down digestion—all things that let us run faster.

Large intestine
completes the process of digestion and absorbs water

Digestion control

Different parts of the digestive system break down food and extract nutrients without us having to think about it. The autonomic nervous system helps to coordinate these processes.

Hypothalamus
regulates the autonomic nervous system and the endocrine system

Cerebellum
helps to control movement, balance, and coordination

Brain stem
helps to control breathing, heart rate, and blood pressure

In control

The autonomic nervous system is controlled by different parts of the brain. The most important of these is the hypothalamus.

Operational control

To control the autonomic nervous system, the brain and spinal cord process information from the body. Then, they send instructions along the nerves of the autonomic nervous system. The hypothalamus is the main area of the brain that regulates this process and also controls different functions of the endocrine system (see pages 26–27).

KEEPING COOL

Temperature control is one of the main jobs of the hypothalamus, which contains special receptors that monitor the body's temperature. One of the most important jobs the autonomic nervous system does is to help keep the body's temperature at a constant 98.6 °F (37 °C). For example, if you start to heat up, the autonomic nervous system makes you sweat, which cools the skin down. It also makes more blood flow near the surface of your skin (allowing the blood to cool down).

Working out

The body can work properly only within a small range of temperatures—if you get too hot or too cold, you become sick. That is why you sweat to keep cool when you exercise.

We remember things, make decisions, and
have opinions

The human brain can think, remember things, make decisions, have opinions, put ideas into words, and plan for the future. The ability to have conscious thoughts like these means that humans are very good at dealing with complicated situations and ideas. It also gives us the ability to read and write, create inventions, and produce works of art. Thinking also means that we are aware that we are individuals, each with our own unique personality.

Investigating the brain

Modern machines, such as this scanner, allow doctors to look at the brain and see if anything is wrong. But we still do not know exactly how it allows us to "think."

How do we think?

Scientists are still not entirely sure how the brain "thinks" or exactly what parts are involved in this complicated process. However, it is clear that the areas of the brain where connections are made between new nerve impulses and stored memories play an important part. The part of the brain that controls speech is also very important (*see opposite page*).

Deep in thought

The brains of these chess players are thinking about how to win the game. To make decisions about their next moves, they are using their knowledge about the rules of chess, which they have had to learn.

Premotor cortex
controls precise movements, such
as using a video game machine

Motor cortex
controls muscle
movements

Broca's center
is the speech
center of the brain

Frontal lobe
controls movements,
speech, and thought

Prefrontal cortex
plays a part in thought,
decision-making,
and planning

Cerebellum
(see page 13)

Frontal lobes

The frontal lobes (located at the front of the cerebral cortex) are one of the most important parts of the brain. They are involved in thinking, planning, and the control of certain types of behavior. The frontal lobes receive nerve impulses from the rest of the brain and are closely linked to the limbic system, which is the center of our emotions (*see pages 22–23*). It is also thought that one part of this lobe (the prefrontal cortex) plays a very important part in determining what kind of people we are—our personalities.

Frontal lobe (left side)

The frontal lobe is divided into four separate areas: the prefrontal cortex, the premotor cortex, the motor cortex, and Broca's center.

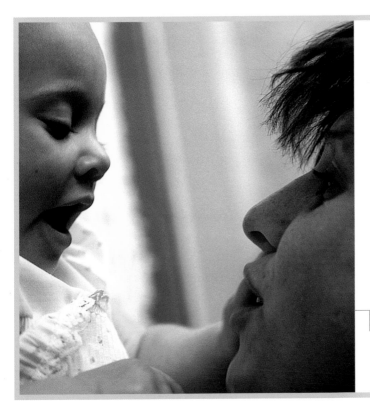

SPEECH

Words and language are a very important part of thinking. You can form words "inside your head" and therefore shape your thoughts. The ability to speak is partly controlled by an area of the brain, called Broca's center, which is located toward the front and on the side of the cerebral cortex. This part of the brain is linked to the motor area of the cerebral cortex that controls the muscles in the mouth, throat, and chest that enable you to talk.

Learning to talk

This baby watches its mother's mouth as part of the process of learning to talk. When we want to tell people what we are thinking, we turn our thoughts into speech.

The limbic system helps
produce emotions

Fear, pleasure, sadness, and anger are just some of the feelings that we can experience. These emotions are very important because they help us to survive and make life exciting. It is thought that they are produced mainly by certain areas of the brain that form a ring, or network, inside the cerebrum. This network is called the limbic system.

Thalamus
sends nerve impulses to the cerebral cortex (*see page 12*)

Hypothalamus
helps control the autonomic nervous system and the endocrine system

Cerebrum
processes information (*see page 13*)

Olfactory bulb
links the sense of smell to memory

Hippocampus
helps to create memories (*see page 25*)

Amygdala
is thought to produce emotional "feelings"

The limbic system

The limbic system not only controls emotions, but also triggers impulses to do things.

The limbic system

The limbic system is made up of structures, such as the amygdala and the hippocampus, linked with the hypothalamus. Little is known about how the limbic system works. However, it is clear that the structures are connected and work with other parts of the brain, such as the "thinking" areas in the frontal lobe and the parts that are linked to memory, to give our thoughts their emotional content.

Basic emotion

Fear is one of the most basic emotions we feel, and it is very important because it helps us protect ourselves from danger. The way in which we feel fear gives an idea of how the limbic system works.

It is thought that the area of the brain that produces the feeling of fear is the amygdala. The amygdala receives sensory information—for example, the sight of a scary place, such as a dark room—and recognizes that it could mean "danger." It then sends nerve impulses that, for example, make the stomach "lurch" with fear and help prepare the body to react.

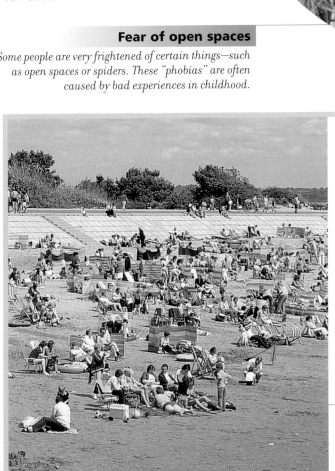

Fear of open spaces

Some people are very frightened of certain things—such as open spaces or spiders. These "phobias" are often caused by bad experiences in childhood.

THAT SMELL REMINDS ME OF ...

Have you ever sensed a smell and almost immediately remembered something that happened to you, or felt a very strong emotion? For example, does the smell of sunscreen remind you of a vacation? This type of experience occurs because the nerves that carry information about smell from the nose run close to the areas of the limbic system, which are linked with the creation of emotions and memory. Certain smells can therefore trigger certain memories and emotions.

Smell familiar?

Strong smells, like that of the hot, sandy beach shown here, can trigger memories. Whether they are memories of good or bad times depends on the individual.

We have different types of
memory

All the knowledge and skills we possess have to be learned and then stored as memories. This store of information is vital for the thinking process. Learning happens from infancy as we try things out and acquire new skills. It is thought that learning happens when new connections are made between neurons in the brain.

Sensory memory
The day-to-day sensory information the brain receives is stored only briefly in the memory.

Sensory memory

There are a number of different types of memory. Most of the information the brain gets from the senses is held only in the "sensory memory" for less than a second—enough time for us to know where we are, so that we can move safely.

Short-term memory

Short-term memory lets us remember things—such as the name of something we have to look up in a book—for a few seconds. This kind of memory is used when we put thoughts into words.

Memory transfer

As this child plays, he stores information in his short-term memory. However, if certain actions are repeated, the skills may be transferred to his long-term memory.

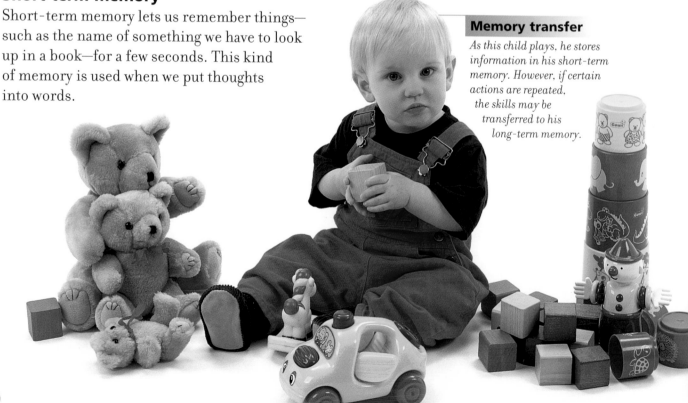

Long-term memory

We store information in the long-term memory by repeating it often. We can keep this information for years, although remembering it can take some time. However, information that is used often from the long-term memory can be remembered quickly. Nobody knows exactly where all the facts and skills we can remember are stored. However, it is thought that the cerebral cortex and the cerebellum are involved, and that the hippocampus (*in the limbic system, see page 22*) helps.

Playing an instrument

When learning a new skill, such as playing a musical instrument, practicing helps us to store it in the long-term memory.

SLEEP AND DREAMS

When you go to sleep, your brain does not stop working. It is not known exactly what the brain does while you sleep, but without it, your brain would have problems thinking and doing things. Scientists believe that sleep is the time when the brain processes the day's events and sorts and stores information. This may be the reason people dream. Brain activity changes through the night (*see below*) as you move through stages of light sleep (colored light blue) and deep sleep (colored dark blue).

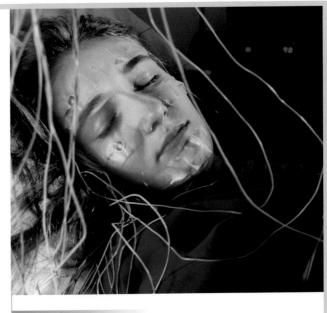

Brain activity

Special machines that are attached to a patient can be used to monitor brain activity during sleep (see below).

Awake

Stages of sleep

| Hours asleep | 1 hour | 2 hours | 3 hours | 4 hours | 5 hours | 6 hours | 7 hours |

The brain is linked to the
endocrine system

The brain controls many of the things that happen in the body through the nervous system. However, the brain is also linked to another system that influences what goes on in the body. This is called the endocrine system.

Chemical messengers

The nervous system uses nerve impulses sent via nerves to carry instructions and information around the body. The endocrine system uses chemicals called hormones. These "chemical messengers" are produced mainly by endocrine glands (*see page 28*). They are carried in the blood to the specific part of the body they affect.

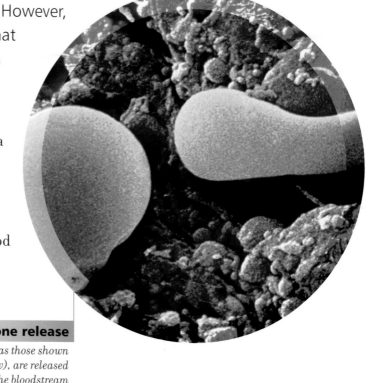

Hormone release

Hormones, such as those shown here (yellow), are released directly into the bloodstream by endocrine glands.

Important functions

The endocrine system controls many different functions in the body, from how the body uses the nutrients in the food we eat, to the production of the sperm and eggs that allows adults to have babies. One of the most important roles of the endocrine system is keeping the chemicals in the body at the right level. For example, the hormones insulin and glucagon are produced by the pancreas and help balance the amount of sugar in the blood at the right level (*see page 29*).

Nutrient management

When we eat food, hormones in the body adjust chemical levels in the blood so they remain balanced.

Hormone release

The brain is linked to the endocrine system, primarily through the hypothalamus. The hypothalamus produces hormones itself and also controls the pituitary gland (to which it is attached). The pituitary gland releases a variety of hormones, some of which control body functions directly. Others control the function of other endocrine glands. For this reason, the pituitary gland is often called the "chief" endocrine gland.

Because the brain and endocrine system are linked, hormones can have an effect on our moods and behavior, while mental processes (such as fear) can affect the production of hormones (*see below*).

Nerve fibers
link the hypothalamus to the pituitary gland

Posterior lobe
stores and releases hormones

Anterior lobe
produces hormones

Blood vessels
transport hormones to the rest of the body in the bloodstream

Pituitary gland (cutaway)

The pituitary gland has two lobes, the anterior (which produces hormones) and the posterior (which stores and releases hormones produced by the hypothalamus).

FIGHT OR FLIGHT

When your brain experiences feelings, such as fear or stress, it sends nerve impulses to the adrenal glands, which produce the hormone adrenaline. Unlike most other hormones, adrenaline is fast-acting and produces a number of effects: it increases heart rate, makes more blood flow to the limbs, and increases the amount of sugar in the blood. All these things prepare the body to fight or run away.

Face off

Adrenaline levels rise as a result of stress, for example, when we cannot find what we want while out shopping. This can lead to heated arguments!

Endocrine glands produce
hormones

Hormones—the body's chemical messengers—are produced in endocrine glands, which release them directly into the blood. The main endocrine glands are the hypothalamus (*see pages 19 and 27*), the pituitary (*see page 27*), the thyroid (which produces the hormone that helps control how the body uses energy it gets from food), the pair of adrenal glands (*see page 27*), the pancreas (*see below*), and the reproductive glands—the ovaries and testes (which produce hormones that control sexual functions).

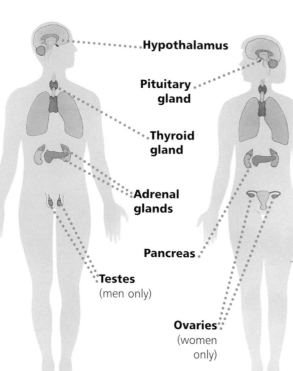

Carrying messages

Some hormones are released at specific times, for example, at the start of puberty. They trigger the production of sperm and eggs.

Cell receptor site

Target cell

Hormone
in the blood

On target

Hormones travel around the body in the blood and, although they reach all the different parts of the body, each hormone makes things happen only in specific tissues. For example, insulin, produced by the pancreas, makes the liver store glucose (a type of sugar that the body gets from food).

Hypothalamus

Pituitary gland

Thyroid gland

Adrenal glands

Pancreas

Testes
(men only)

Ovaries
(women only)

Endocrine glands

Endocrine glands are located all over the body, producing different hormones at different times. These are just some of the glands.

Target lock on

A hormone affects only its "target" tissues. The cells of these tissues have shaped "receptor sites" into which only the hormone's molecules can fit, like a key in a lock.

The feedback loop

The action of hormones is often controlled by a "feedback loop." For example, the rise or fall of glucose levels in the blood is sensed by cells in the pancreas. The pancreas then produces more or less hormones (insulin and glucagon) to bring levels of glucose back to normal. Insulin makes the liver store glucose, while glucagon raises levels of blood glucose because it makes the liver release glucose into the blood.

Pancreas produces more glucagon and less insulin

Blood glucose levels rise

Exercise lowers blood glucose levels

BLOOD GLUCOSE LEVELS NORMAL

Eating raises blood glucose levels

Blood glucose levels fall

Pancreas produces more insulin and less glucagon

Glucose balance

This is just one example of a feedback loop. Each loop ensures that hormones are produced when required and that the levels of hormones remain balanced.

DIABETES

If the glands of the endocrine system malfunction, many things can go wrong. Diabetes is one example of a problem that occurs when the body does not produce a hormone—in this case insulin—properly or if the body's cells do not respond normally to it. With diabetes, blood glucose levels become too high, and the person feels thirsty and hungry, and can lose weight and become tired.

Treating the effects

Diabetes can occur in young people and adults. Its effects can be treated by a regular insulin injection, shown here, and dietary changes.

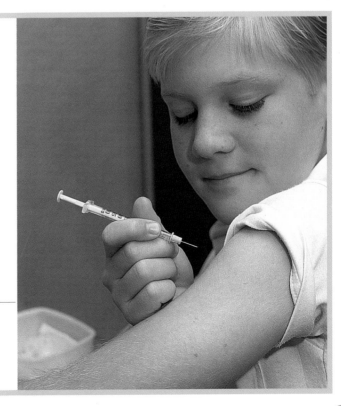

Glossary

Adrenal glands A pair of endocrine glands located on the top of the kidneys. They produce hormones, including adrenaline.

Amygdala A small, almond-shaped structure in the limbic system, thought to produce feelings of fear.

Association neuron A type of neuron that relays impulses from one neuron to another.

Autonomic nervous system The part of the nervous system that automatically controls body functions, such as the heart rate.

Brain The control center of the nervous system, made up of billions of nerve cells.

Brainstem The region where the brain and spinal cord meet. It helps control vital body functions such as heart beat and breathing.

Central nervous system The part of the nervous system that includes the brain and the spinal cord. It coordinates and controls the body.

Cerebellum The part of the brain that controls balance and movement.

Cerebral cortex The surface layer of the cerebrum.

Cerebrum The largest part of the brain that coordinates things such as thoughts and actions.

Dendrite The part of a neuron that carries nerve impulses toward its cell body.

Electroencephalograph (EEG) A machine that measures electrical activity produced by the brain.

Endocrine gland A structure inside the body that produces and secretes hormones directly into the blood.

Endocrine system The system of glands and organs that secrete hormones. It controls many of the basic functions of the body.

Glucagon A hormone secreted by cells in the pancreas that causes the liver to release stored glucose into the blood.

Glucose A type of sugar that the body gets from food.

Gray matter Areas of the central nervous system made up of the cell bodies of neurons, for example, the cerebral cortex.

Hormones Chemicals produced by endocrine glands that alter the activity of various organs in the body. Hormones are "chemical messengers" and are carried by the blood.

Hippocampus A structure in the brain that is involved with the regulation of emotions and the formation of long-term memory.

Hypothalamus A part of the brain that monitors and regulates many basic body functions, such as temperature and water balance.

Insulin A hormone secreted by cells in the pancreas that causes the body to store glucose.

Limbic system A group of brain structures that work to help regulate emotion and memory.

Motor neuron A type of neuron that carries nerve impulses from the brain and spinal cord to muscles or organs.

Nerve A bundle of nerve fibers.

Nerve impulse An electrical signal that travels along a neuron. Nerve impulses carry information and instructions around the nervous system.

Neuron A nerve cell that carries nerve impulses. Billions of neurons make up the nervous system.

Pancreas A gland that is part of the digestive system. It contains cells that produce the hormones insulin and glucagon.

Peripheral nervous system The part of the nervous system made up of nerves that connects the brain and spinal cord to the rest of the body.

Pituitary gland An important endocrine gland that produces a number of hormones, some of which control body functions.

Sensory neuron A type of neuron that carries nerve impulses to the brain and spinal cord from sensory receptors in the sense organs and other parts of the body.

Soft tissue "Soft" areas of the body not made up of bone and cartilage, such as the brain,

Spinal cord The tube of nerve tissue that runs down the back of the body from the base of the brain to the lower back. It is the main communication route between the brain and the rest of the body.

Synapse A junction between two neurons or between a neuron and muscle fiber. The synapse contains a small gap across which chemicals can flow to "pass on" nerve impulses.

Thyroid gland An endocrine gland found in the neck that produces hormones that, for example, stimulate growth.

White matter Areas of the central nervous system made up of nerve fibers.

Find out more

These are just some of the Web sites where you can find more information about the human brain. Many of the sites also provide information and illustrations about other systems and processes of the human body.

www.dana.org
A Web site from the Dana Foundation, featuring a brainy kids section where you can link directly to other brain-related sites.

www.biausa.org/Pages/for_kids.html
Child-friendly section of the Brain Injury Association of America, featuring information about brain injuries and Web links.

www.kidshealth.org
Find a lot of information on this site about all the different parts of the body—including the brain—and how to keep them healthy.

http://faculty.washington.edu/chudler/neurok.html
A Web site covering everything from keeping your brain healthy to understanding how it works.

http://pfizer.com/brain
Play brain-related games on this Web site from Pfizer Inc.

www.brainaustralia.org.au
Discover more information about how to keep your brain healthy on this site from the Australian Brain Foundation.

www.bbc.co.uk/science/humanbody
A Web site devoted to all parts of the body, including the brain. Find out how it works, play mind games, and take the personality test.

http://hendrix.ei.dtu.dk
Web site of THOR Center for Neuroinformatics, Denmark, featuring mini movies of brain activity.

www.whonamedit.com/doctor.cfm/1982.htm
Find out more about French scientist Pierre Broca and his attempts to map the brain.

www.medtropolis.com/VBody.asp
Look at different parts of the brain on this virtual tour.

Index